DATE DUE

JU

SAVING MONEY

by Tanya Thayer

Glenview Public Library
1930 Glenview Road
Glenview, Illinois

Lerner Publications Company · Minneapolis

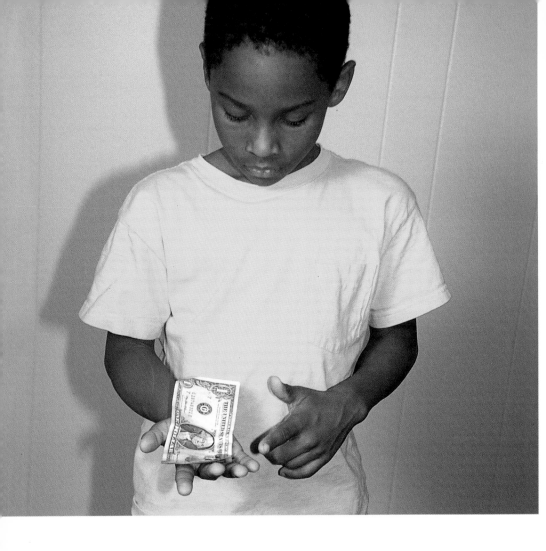

I can **save money.**

When I keep money,
I save it.

I can save a little
bit of money.

I can save money in a jar.

I can save money
to **buy** gum.

I can save money
to buy a soda.

I can save money
to buy a book.

I can save money
to buy a ball.

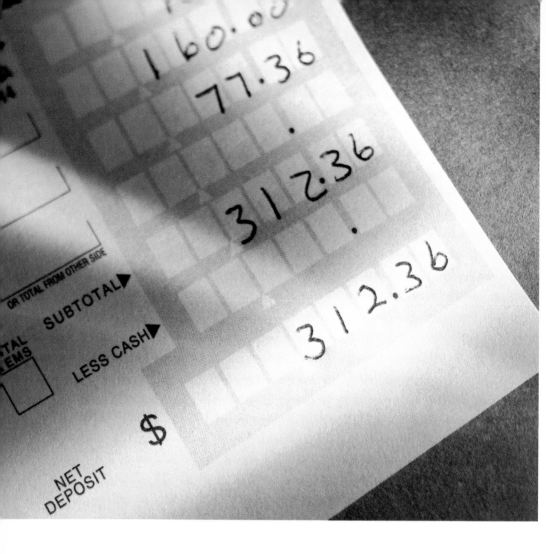

I can save a lot of money.

I can save money
in a **bank.**

I can save money
for a party.

I can save money
to buy a bike.

I can save money
for a pet.

I can save money
to buy a toy car.

I can keep my money until
I know what I want.

I save money when I don't
buy anything at all.

Where can I save money?

There are many places where you can save a little bit of money. You can save money in a jar, in a piggy bank, or in a special place in your room.

When you save a lot of money, a safe place to keep it is in a bank. The bank will send you a letter every month to tell you how much money you have saved.

Saving Money Facts

 The first bank in the United States opened in 1781 in Philadelphia, Pennsylvania.

 Piggy banks were originally made from a clay called pygg. Later the banks were made to look like pigs and were called piggy banks.

Save your money for a rainy day. What does this saying mean? It means you keep some extra money for a later time when you need it.

 A penny saved is a penny earned. What does this saying mean? It means that it is hard work saving money, but the more you save the more you will have.

Glossary

 bank – a safe place to keep money

 buy – to give money for something

 money – what people use to buy things

 save – to put away and keep

Index

The photographs in this book are reproduced through the courtesy of: Corbis Royalty Free, front cover, 3, 5, 10, 17, 22 (2nd from bottom), 22 (bottom); © N. Alexander/Visuals Unlimited, 2; Todd Strand/IPS, 4, 8; © D. Yeske/Visuals Unlimited, 6, 22 (2nd from top); © Earl & Nazima Kowall/CORBIS, 7; © Eric Anderson/Visuals Unlimited, 9; © Ryan McVay, 11, 19 (top); Stockbyte, 12; © Robert Trubia/CORBIS, 13; ©Laura Dwight/ CORBIS, 14; © Jeff Greenberg/Visuals Unlimited, 15; © Sara J. Cross/Visuals Unlimited, 16; Beth Osthoff/IPS, 19 (bottom), 22, (top).

Lerner Publications Company
A division of Lerner Publishing Group
241 First Avenue North
Minneapolis, MN 55401 U.S.A.

Website address: www.lernerbooks.com

Library of Congress Cataloging-in-Publication Data

Thayer, Tanya.
        Saving money / by Tanya Thayer.
            p.   cm. — (First step nonfiction)
        Includes index.
        Summary: Presents the concept of saving money and items for which a young child might save, such as gum, a book, or even a car.
        ISBN: 0–8225–1260–2 (lib. bdg. : alk. paper)
        1. Saving and investment—Juvenile literature. 2. Children—Finance, Personal—Juvenile literature. [1. Saving and investment. 2. Finance, Personal.] I. Title. II. Series.
        HB822 .T43 2002
        332.024'01—dc21   2001002451

Manufactured in the United States of America
1 2 3 4 5 6 – AM – 07 06 05 04 03 02